# MOUNTAIN GORILLAS

## TEXT AND PHOTOGRAPHS
## BY JULIE CONNAL

This is a mountain gorilla. His name is Marcel. Marcel and his family group live high in the mountains of Zaire, a country that forms part of the *continent* of Africa.

The mountain gorillas' diet is vegetarian and includes such foods as the leaves, stalks, and shoots of plants. Much of a gorilla's day is spent looking for food and resting. A family group may travel as much as a mile between several feeding sessions each day.

At nightfall each gorilla builds a sleeping nest from branches and *foliage*. A new nest is built each night and is constructed either on the ground or in the trees.

Mother gorillas carry their babies around on their backs for the first three months of their lives. The baby gorilla sleeps in its mother's nest at night and rides on her back during the day.

The young gorillas are playful and have a lot of fun running, rolling, tumbling, and climbing in their jungle home.

Mountain gorillas are *rare*, so they are an *endangered* species. These gorillas are rare for two main reasons. First, they have lost much of their natural *habitat*, the jungle, as a result of farming. Second, they have been killed by *poachers*–people who hunt illegally.

Mountain gorillas must be protected from *extinction* and the threat of poachers. For this reason, the areas that mountain gorillas live in are *designated* as national parks and are closely guarded and watched by park rangers.

Small groups of people trek into the jungle each day to see the gorillas and sit with them for a while. Park rangers tell the visitors that they must be quiet and not get too close to the gorillas.

Staying away is hard, because the young gorillas are curious and want to come close!

It is very important that the gorillas are looked after and protected in their habitat so that they can continue to flourish and we can enjoy them for years to come.

Glossary

continent–a land mass

designated–set apart

endangered–at risk

extinction–completely dying out

foliage–leaves of a tree or plant

habitat–a natural environment

poachers–people who hunt illegally

rare–uncommon